LEARNING BASH
Shell Scripting
Gently

Sujata Biswas

CONTENTS

LEARNING SHELL SCRIPTING GENTLY

With the automation menace hovering over us, it is imperative that we equip ourselves with skills that can preserve our jobs for the years to come.

The competition is tough. IT Industry experts express concern that 60% of IT workers may lose their jobs. However, it is not that we do not face challenges now. After a certain age, the ability to absorb new skills gradually diminishes, it would not have mattered say 20 years back. However, now, experienced folks are not seen as assets in a company but merely as units for which the company pays a certain amount of money. The prevailing idea is why not get the job done by a fresher/intern! There is a dip in quality, but that is ok. In such a scenario, it becomes important that we bring value to our jobs by learning new technologies and if they do not appreciate it, then, well, we can always search for greener pastures. Shell Scripting in Linux is my response to the threat of automation. Let's confront the fears that haunt us and get on with it. I am sure we can ride this so-called wave of automation with better skills and better quality of life for our families.

TARGET AUDIENCE:

You should have some experience in working through your way on Linux or similar Operating Systems. The goal is to get your scripting knowledge to such a level that you can easily jump to Scripting/Programming Languages such as Python, TCL/TK. It is not the end but the beginning of learning. Many concepts are repeated throughout the book. The Target is to get you understand the concepts and lay a strong foundation.

CHAPTER 1: GOING THRU LINUX FUNDAMENTALS

What is BASH?

BASH stands for Bourne Again Shell. This shell is also present in other Operating Systems such as Linux, Mint, etc.

If you learn BASH scripting here, you should have no problem porting your scripts to another Operating System. BASH is almost universal.

Simply put, at the heart of your Linux Operating System is the Kernel. The Kernel is THE Linux and provides an abstraction layer between you and hardware components of the system. The shell surrounds the kernel and provides you, the user, access to the Kernel.

Connect to an Ubuntu/Linux System, whether by **ssh** or **telnet**. Provide the username and password. You see something like:

$

It is called the shell prompt.

Now type the following command:

$ cat /etc/issue
Ubuntu 16.04.1 LTS \n \l

The **cat** is an Ubuntu/Linux command which displays the content of an ASCII file called **issue**. The first **/** is the root, the, **etc** is a directory inside the root while **issue** is the filename whose contents are displayed; showing the release of the Ubuntu Operating System, which, in this case, is 16.04.

16.04 refers to the year and the month. While LTS stands for Long Term Support.

To check if your shell is BASH, you can enter the following command:

$ echo $SHELL

$ echo $SHELL
/bin/bash

The echo command displays the value of the environment variable SHELL. Variables are placeholders in the memory that contain a value. In this case, the value is the **/bin/bash**. The first **/** is the **root**, the **bin** is a directory, while **bash** is executable. Since the whole path is presented from the root, this is called an Absolute Path.

What are streams?

You must understand or at least revise streams. There are three streams in Ubuntu/Linux:

Input: What you type on the shell prompt. Also, called **stdin.**

Output: What the shell reverts to you. Also, called **stdout**.

Error: The error message the shell reverts to you. Also, called **stderr.**

Streams are numerically represented in the following manner:

stdin 0

stdout 1

stderr 2

Note: Stream is an important concept.

Let us enter a command to check the System Level we are in. The command we use is **who -r**, which is the input stream

$ who -r

> **run-level 5 2017-02-25 14:20**

run-level 5 2017-02-25 14:20 is the Output stream.

The error message 2 (stderr) is useful in shell scripting. In most scripts, we are dealing with TRUE and FALSE. Suppose, there is a script that on encountering an error should give an error message like echo "This command failed to run". However, you do not want the error message thrown by the script to appear on the standard output (screen). It is better to redirect the error message to an endless hole called **/dev/null**. You learn more about redirection in the next section.

Do **ls -l** on a non-existent file:

$ ls -l nofile.txt

ls: cannot access 'nofile.txt': No such file or directory

Suppose, this error message is useless because you want to give an Error message of your own. Then, what should do you do? Remember, there are many tests where you want some condition to fail as well.

$ ls -l nofile.txt 2>/dev/null

$

This simply means that in case of error, the error message, signified by 2, should go to /**dev/null** file (and not display on the Standard Output or your screen).

If the error message is something that you need in future, for example, system logs, etc. Then you can simply direct the error message to a file.

$ ls -l nofile.txt 2> error.log

#Blank next line

$

$ cat error.log

ls: cannot access 'nofile.txt': No such file or directory

What is Redirection?

Redirection is sending the output to a file instead of showing it on the screen.

$ who -u

peter tty7   2017-02-25 14:20 old   1136 (:0)

bobbydeb pts/19   2017-02-26 14:17 .   10967 (192.168.1.2)

The **who** command along with **-u** operator DISPLAYS the output on the screen.

who -u #<- STDIN

The output or STDOUT is

peter tty7   2017-02-25 14:20 old   1136 (:0)

bobbydeb pts/19   2017-02-26 14:17 .   10967 (192.168.1.2)

The standard output can be anything from a file to a printer. To redirect the output of **who -u** to a file, use the > and the file name. There is no output on the screen because the output goes to a file

$ who -u > /tmp/userslist

$

See, there is no response from the shell. The output is redirected to a file called **userslist** (or any name you prefer) in the tmp directory in the root **/** . To check the contents of **userslist**, type the **cat** command and the absolute path to **userslist**

cat /tmp/userslist

$ cat /tmp/userslist

peter tty7   2017-02-25 14:20 old   1136 (:0)

bobbydeb pts/19   2017-02-26 14:17 .   10967 (192.168.1.2)

Note: You do not have to have the file **userslist** before running the example. The file, if it does not exist, is created. If it already exists, then the old data is overwritten, so use >> to append content.

For instance, let us redirect the output of **who -r** to **userslist** file.

$ who -r >> /tmp/userslist

Tip: Look at the third line.

$ cat /tmp/userslist

peter   tty7   2017-02-25 14:20 (:0)

bobbydeb pts/19   2017-02-26 14:17 (192.168.1.2)

**   run-level 5 2017-02-25 14:20**

Explain Permissions

Everything in Ubuntu/Linux is a file. We deal with two file types:

- Files
- Directories

Run the **ls -l** command, which displays the contents of a directory. A directory may have several subdirectories and files as well. We use the **ls -l** to check contents. Look at the first column and mentally divide the output you see into 4 sections in the ratio of 1:3:3:3.

$ ls -l

total 16

drwxrwxr-x 2 bobbydeb bobbydeb 4096 Feb 26 16:10 testDIR

-rw-rw-r-- 1 bobbydeb bobbydeb   0 Feb 26 16:10 testFILE

Identifying a directory and its permissions:

drwxrwxr-x 2 bobbydeb bobbydeb 4096 Feb 26 16:10 testDIR

drwxrwxr-x

d means directory. So testDIR is a directory. If it were - (dash), it would be a file. Let us now divide the next 9 characters:

rwx : Reads that the owner bobbydeb has read/write/execute permissions.

rwx : Reads that the group bobbydeb has read/write/execute permissions.

r-x : Reads that rest of the world has only read and execute permissions.

Note: In this example names of the user and the group are same. So, don't get confused. This is a default behavior where Linux creates same username and group name.

Identifying file permissions:

-rw-rw-r-- 1 bobbydeb bobbydeb   0 Feb 26 16:10 testFILE

-rw-rw-r--

- means that it is a file.

rw- : Reads that the owner bobbydeb has read/write permissions.

rw- : Reads that the group bobbydeb has read/write permissions.

r-- : Reads that rest of the world has only read permission.

You must give the file's owner, EXECUTE permission, otherwise, the bash script files will not run. You should use the command **chmod**.

Before applying **chmod**, see how the permissions look for the file **testFILE**

-rw-rw-r-- 1 bobbydeb bobbydeb   0 Feb 26 16:10 testFILE

Applying the **chmod** command with operators u , + and x. Basically, you are "giving" (adding) the owner, bobbydeb, execute permission represented by x.

$ chmod u+x testFILE

Note: Run the command chmod u+x <filename.sh> before trying out your scripts.

Now, perform ls -l on testFILE and see the difference.

$ ls -l testFILE

-rwxrw-r-- 1 bobbydeb bobbydeb 0 Feb 26 16:10 testFILE

Tip: To see if the command is successfully executed or not, check the value of an in-built variable: echo $?. This is called the EXIT STATUS. Any value other ZERO means the preceding command was unsuccessful:

$ echo $?
0

What are Variables?

A variable holds a value. The value can be changed. Hence, the value of a variable is temporary. Relate a variable with the memory, do not confuse it with a file – which resides on your hard disk.

You define the variable in the following manner.

$ Example=Ubun2017

To check the value of the variable called **Example**, type the command:

$ echo $Example

Note: The first **$** is prompt.

The variable **Example** has the value **Ubun2017** which is a remote system. Let us assume a case where a client application is programmed to look at the variable **Example** to know the name of the remote system for some services it needs. Now, suppose the machine **Ubun2017** suffers a hardware breakdown, and you prepared a new remote server to replace it.

The client application fails to work unless the value of **Example** is changed to the new value.

$ Example=Ubun2018

Now, the client application works again with the new value.

You may remove the value of the variable using the **unset** command.

$ unset Example

To perform mathematical expressions with variables, you can assign a number to the variable, but it has a different format:

$ num=100

$ echo $((num))

The value is still 100, but this construct can be used to perform mathematical calculations, for instance:

$ echo $((num + 300))

400

Variables are reusable as well. Here's an example, we define a variable called **filenames** with values filename1 filename2 filename3 filename4 filename5. Use double quotes so that the shell thinks it is the same string. Remember, even the whitespace is of some meaning to the Shell, the double quotes negate their meaning, so it must be used. The shell expects a single word for the variable value.

$filenames="filename1 filename2 filename3 filename4 filename5"

$ echo $filenames
filename1 filename2 filename3 filename4 filename5

Note: Use the **touch** command to create files using the value of the filenames

$ touch $filenames

Check using **ls** command:

$ ls filename*
filename1 filename2 filename3 filename4 filename5

Hence, this variable filename can be used across the system to create these files. You do not have to remember the filenames, just the variable name.

Tip: A variable cannot start with a Number. This applies to other scripting and programming languages as well. Look at the error; shell gives when you try to assign a variable starting with a number to the value hello.

$ 99=hello

99=hello: command not found

CHAPTER 2 : LOCAL VARIABLES VERSUS ENVIRONMENT VARIABLES

Double or Single Quotes?

Before we embark on understanding variables, it is important to know about the differences between double and single quotes and also touch upon other topics as well.

Put **5** as variable's **abc** 's value

$ abc=5

Now, you know you can display the value of **abc** with the **echo** command.

$ echo $abc

$ 5

This is the default behavior of the shell, and is called variable expansion and is same if you put **abc** with double quotes – the shell allows variable expansion.

$ echo "$abc"

However, if you enclose the variable **abc** with **single quotes,** you see **no** variable expansion. **Therefore, use single quotes when you want to preserve the sanctity of the text**.

$ echo '$abc'

$ abc

Note: Due to formatting differences, single quotes and double may appear different visually.

As you deal with variables in shell programming, it is imperative to understand the difference between Local variables and Environment variables.

Note: Local Variables are also called Shell Variables.

What are Local Variables?

In short, the value of the local variable is only applicable to the current shell. In the following example, we define a variable called height and value it to 5. The value of the variable is stored as a string (text). The value of the height is 5. However, when you enter the command **bash** to open different instance of the shell, the value of height is empty. Thus, the value of a local variable is NOT inherited.

$ height=5

$ echo $height

5

$ bash #This is the command to open another shell instance

$ echo $height

$

To turn local or shell variable into Environment Variable use the **export** command.

Check if the Local variable height and its value exist:

$echo height

5

Yes, it does. To turn this variable to an Environment variable, **export** the **height** variable:

$ export height

Now, open another instance of bash
$ bash

Check the value of the height variable:

$ echo $height

Yes, the value is 5. A more technical way of saying this can be that the Shell expands the variable and what you get to see is the value of the variable.

It is important to know the difference between local and environment variables. It is a popular Interview Question for beginners.

What are Variable brace expansions?

Administrators use brace expansions to copy files from one location to another. Many software applications generate files which have similar names apart from few differences. For instance, consider the following files in the directory:

$ ls

backup helloA helloB helloC helloD

$ cp hello{A,B,C,D} backup/

Where hello{A,B,C,D) expands to helloA, helloB, helloC, helloD and backup/ is the directory. It is an over-simplistic example, but this is how brace expansions are popularly used.

Even this command works:

$cp hello{A..D} backup/

The consecutive expansive takes place {A..D} expanding to A, B, C, and D. It exhibits the same behavior if you use numbers as well.

How to perform Mathematical Calculations on the Shell?

The commonly used mathematical expansions used on the shell is performed using brackets.

In the following examples, **echo** is used to calculate multiplication of 78 x 78 with double brackets; **echo** throws the standard output 6048. You can also see how a variable called multiply is given the value of 6048.

$ echo $((78 * 78))

6084

$multiply=$((78 * 78))

$echo $multiply

$6048

You encounter mathematical expressions later in the book as well.

Command Substitutions

Learning about command substitution is important for future lessons. The syntax is simple enough

$variable=$(command)

Or

$variable=`command`

(Using backticks NOT single quotes)

$ echo "The disk space in $(du -sk)"

The disk space in 30852 .

Consider the following example, in this example the output of **uname -a** is fed to the awk command. The **awk** considers tab its natural delimiter and thus the first field is taken out from the output of the **uname -a** command.

$uname -a

Linux linuxmachine 4.4.0-78-generic #99-Ubuntu SMP Thu Apr 27 15:29:09 UTC 2017 x86_64 x86_64 x86_64 GNU/Linux

$1 – Linux is the First Column

$2 – linuxmachine is the Second Column

Subsequently, the separators are ever-changing, so the syntax of the **awk** command will change too. This is a rudimentary introduction to **awk**, which is a scripting language as well.

Note: There is a chapter devoted to **awk** entirely.

$echo " The operating system is `uname -a | awk '{print $1}'` "

The operating system is Linux #Output

They have a special role to play in shell scripting as the command outputs are routinely captured for further processing. It is a good idea to perfect this sub-topic. The previous command line is put as a value to a variable.

CHAPTER 3 :
CUSTOMIZING YOUR
ENVIRONMENT

It is important to understand two concepts. In Linux and other operating systems, there is something called universal and personal settings. In a company, everybody gets a salary; this is a universal item. However, not everybody gets the same salary. Your Boss obviously gets a different salary than you. Similarly, there are some common settings applicable to all users, and there are personal settings that are only applicable to you. In Linux/Ubuntu environment the Universal settings are called System-wide settings. These settings apply to all users in the system via some script files.

The first file, containing series of commands and calls to other files is the PROFILE file. It exists in **/etc** directory. Don't worry about the details mentioned in the file. It is easier to read, really! The code blocks talk about setting the prompt (PS) depending upon the shell you login to. There is a call to execute another file called **bash.bashrc**.

/etc/profile: system-wide .profile file for the Bourne shell (sh(1))

and Bourne compatible shells (bash(1), ksh(1), ash(1), ...).

if ["$PS1"]; then

  if ["$BASH"] && ["$BASH" != "/bin/sh"]; then

    # The file bash.bashrc already sets the default PS1.

/etc/profile: system-wide .profile file for the Bourne shell (sh(1))

and Bourne compatible shells (bash(1), ksh(1), ash(1), ...).

if ["$PS1"]; then

  if ["$BASH"] && ["$BASH" != "/bin/sh"]; then

    # The file bash.bashrc already sets the default PS1.

    # PS1='\h:\w\$ '

    if [-f /etc/bash.bashrc]; then

     . /etc/bash.bashrc

   fi

  else

   if ["`id -u`" -eq 0]; then

    PS1='#'

   else

    PS1='$'

   fi

  fi

fi

Note: Come back when you have read this book twice and see if you can understand the script.

The second file or a set of files that get executed by the shell for system-wide settings exists in the **/etc/profile.d** directory.

What are Personal Settings?

In the last section, we identified **/etc/profile** and scripts kept in **/etc/profile.d** are executed first when a user logins. The three files for personal settings are:

- **.bash_profile** (Read as DOT BASH Underscore Profile)
- **.bash_login** (Read as DOT Bash Underscore Login)
- **.profile** (Read as Dot Profile)

And,

.bashrc (Read as DOT BASH RC)

These files (or at least some of them) are found in your home directory.

If you put a dot at the beginning of the file. That file becomes hidden and can only be listed using the **ls -al** :

.bash_history .bash_logout .bashrc .profile .python_history

These are the files in my directory. Notice that I do not have **.bash_profile** and **.bash_login**. However, that does not matter, **.profile** is enough. I do not have **.bashrc** as well. If in your case, you have all the three files, **.bash_profile**, **.bash_login** and **.profile**. The execution precedence is **.bash_profile**, the shell ignores **.bash_login** and **.profile** files.

The reason you may not have these files lies with the **useradd** command when you are creating users.

The **.bash_profile** calls the **.bashrc file**. The **.bashrc** file contains aliases and functions. Let's what you can do with the **.profile** file.

The following are the last lines of .profile

set PATH so it includes user's private bin directories
PATH="$HOME/bin:$HOME/.local/bin:$PATH"

Using your favorite editor, put the **date** command after the **PATH** and login again. You see that the **date** command is executed once you have entered your login name and password. You can do things on the fly as well. For instance, let's try and change the **PATH** variable.

Check the current value of the **PATH** variable using the **echo** command

$ echo $PATH
/usr/local/sbin:/usr/local/bin:/usr/sbin:/usr/bin:/sbin:/bin:/usr/games:/usr/local/games

Open .**profile** in your favorite editor and add the following text:

PATH="$HOME/bin:$HOME/.local/bin:$PATH"

TO

PATH="$HOME/bin:$HOME/.local/bin:$PATH:/home/bobbydeb/justlikethat"

Save. Back to the prompt.

To re-initialize the .profile, in other words, to source it for the current shell. You have two choices

$ . .profile

Or

$ source .profile

Then check the PATH variable.

$ echo $PATH

/usr/local/sbin:/usr/local/bin:/usr/sbin:/usr/bin:/sbin:/bin:/ usr/games:/usr/local/games/home/bobbydeb/justlikethat

Note: If you have both **.bash_profile** and **.profile** files in your home directory, then .bash_profile will be executed.

What is .bashrc file?

The **.bashrc** stores list of command shortcuts by using the **alias** command. There would be some aliases already created by the system.

 # some more ls aliases

alias ll='ls -alF'

alias la='ls -A'

alias l='ls -CF'

If you enter **ll** or **la** or **l**, the **ls** command with the corresponding options runs. If you want to check the aliases in your current shell without opening the **.bashrc** file, then simply enter the **alias** command on the prompt.

$ alias

alias alert='notify-send --urgency=low -i "$([$? = 0] && echo terminal || echo error)" "$(history|tail -n1|sed -e '\"s/^\s*[0-9]\+ \s*//;s/[;&|]\s*alert$//'\")'"
alias egrep='egrep --color=auto'
alias fgrep='fgrep --color=auto'
alias grep='grep --color=auto'
alias l='ls -CF'
alias la='ls -A'
alias ll='ls -alF'
alias ls='ls --color=auto'

CHAPTER 4 : SHELL FEATURES

Command Structure

The command structure followed by Linux is

command agrument1 arugument2
For example, if we want to rename a file called hello to bye. The command is:

$ mv hello bye

mv is a command, from the shell scripting point it can also be the argument 0 (Zero), **hello** is the first argument while **bye** is the second argument.

Command options

For example, we want to see all the hidden files in a directory; the command is:

$ ls -a

While **ls** is the command, **-a** is an option.

What is the Path Variable?

The Path is an important variable. If Path variable is absent, you would not be able to run any commands on the command line. It is a variable that the Shell looks into to execute the binaries that you have typed on the prompt. The value of the Path variable is a list of directories delimited by a colon.

To look the value of the path variable (or any variable for that matter), type

$echo $PATH

/usr/lib64/qt-3.3/bin:/usr/local/bin:/bin:/usr/sbin:/sbin

CHAPTER 5: EXIT STATUS WITH AND AND OR OPERATORS

Linux shell offers exit status for you to know whether your last command is successful or not. The exit status of ZERO means your command has executed successfully, while any NON-ZERO value from 1 to 255 indicates that your command is unsuccessful.

Let us create two files called **test1** and **test2** using the touch command. When you enter touch command followed by a file name, it creates a new file, if the file does not exist. However, if the file exists, the modification time of the file is changed. Test this using ls -l command.

$ touch test1

If now, you do echo $?, you see a Zero in the output. The $? is a special variable that stores the exit status of the preceding command.

Now type:

$ touch TYPE2

Since Linux is case sensitive, the TYPE2 file is treated differently. However, we have not yet created the TEST2 file.

$ ls TEST2

ls: cannot access TEST2: No such file or directory

You get an error message. Now enter, **echo $?**

What do you see? You see a NON-ZERO value. In Ubuntu, you may see 2 while in Centos you may see 127. All you need to know is that you have got a NON-ZERO value indicating that the command was unsuccessful.

Most of Linux commands, even built-in binaries, would have exit status in their code. In fact, most of the commands have a section for Exit status in their manual (use the man command followed by the command, like **$ man ls**) pages.

AND operator

The AND operator is symbolized by the && on Linux.

Syntax:

command_1 && command_2

Here, **command_2** executes when if **command_1** successfully executes.

How does the Shell know the first command was successful?

Read the **$?** Variable and check if the exit value is ZERO. If command_1 is not successful, command_2 does not execute.

Steps:

Create a file using cat > <filename>

cat > exam1

Start typing content and enter **Control + d** .

$cat exam1

$ls exam1 && cat exam1

$ ls exam1 && cat exam1

exam1

Hello, My name is John

In OR operator, the second command executes only if the first command returns failure or Non-ZERO exit status. The OR operator is symbolized with

|| .

Steps:

We do a **ls** on the non-existent file called exam2; we see that echo **$?** has returned a Non-Zero value which is expected.

$ ls exam2

ls: cannot access 'exam2': No such file or directory

$ echo $?

2

Now, using OR operator which works on the principle that if the first command has failed, then the second command succeeds:

$ ls exam2 || cat exam1

ls: cannot access 'exam2': No such file or directory

Hello, My name is John

The output of the second command is, of course, Hello, My name is John . Alternately, if you run **ls** against exam1 (which exists), the OR operator's real power is displayed.

$ls exam1 || cat exam1

What is the output? Do you see "Hello, My name is John" - the content of exam1?

$ ls exam1 || cat exam1

exam1

As you see, the content of **exam1** with **cat** is not displayed. This is because the first command has succeeded, invalidating the second command because of the OR operator ||.

CHAPTER 6 : ESCAPING CHARACTERS

Escaping special meaning of some characters is an important concept.

Let us see the value of a variable

$ echo $FOO

$

We see that nothing has been returned. This is because no value has been assigned to the FOO variable. When shell sees $ it attaches a special meaning to it.

The string preceding $ is seen as a variable. But what if we want to see just $FOO , like

$echo Hello

Which returns

$Hello

The way to return $FOO is to destroy the meaning of $ by prefixing it with \ (forward slash)

$echo "\$FOO"

Moreover, now you get the expected $FOO; another way is to use single quotes, which leaves the string intact, negating any special values as well.

$echo '$FOO'

You may also give the output of the Linux commands as a value to variables. Run the command date:

$ date
Sun May 28 22:10:16 IST 2017

You have to use backticks. In fact, backtick is also called command substitution. To send the output of the date command to a variable,

Enter:

$ a=`date`

Note: It is backticks and not single quotes. The backtick symbol is above the TAB key of your keyboard.

$ echo $a
Sun May 28 22:10:16 IST 2017

Another way to put the command output to a variable is using the following syntax:

$b=$(who -r)
run-level 5 2017-05-27 15:46

CHAPTER 7 :
THE COMMAND
INTERPRETER

Let us write the first script. It is considered lucky to start it with the Universal "Hello World" program. We do not want to break the tradition; we create the first program.

Steps to create the first program:

$vi first.sh

Type the content after pressing the small i key and then save by pressing Keyboard escape and wq! to save and exit.

echo "Hello World"

x=5

echo $x

Note: The second line defines a variable called **x** and assigns it to **5**. Moreover, then echoes back the value of **x**.

When you return back to the prompt, give the execute (x) permission for the user (u):

$chmod u+x first.sh

run the command:
$./first.sh

$ ./first.sh
Hello World
5

Congrats, this may be the first program you have created. Now, let us make this program fail by changing the shell from current Bash to Csh (C - shell).

To check the current shell, SHELL is an IN-BUILT environment variable
$echo $SHELL

$/bin/bash

/bin/bash is the value that the shell returns, implying that you are using BASH as the command interpreter. A command interpreter translates your scripts to a language understandable to the computer. Coming back to the subject, if the following line is not in your script

!#/bin/bash

Note: !#/bin/bash is called SHABANG, is the first line of the script.

Even without this line, the script executes in your current shell but may fail or behave differently in other shells. Hence, please include this line before typing your code. Ideally, **first.sh** should look like:

```
#!/bin/bash
#This program echoes Hello World string, assigns a value to a variable to x and then displays it.
echo "Hello World"
x=5
echo $x
```

Note: The Industry practice is to put comments after # . However, for new learners, it creates a busy visual experience leading to confusion. Avoid commenting during the learning stage.

CHAPTER 8 :
INTERACT WITH
USERS USING READ

Writing interactive scripts is easy in Bash scripting..

To get more information about **read**, enter

$type read

read is a shell builtin

moreover, for more information on **read**, use:

$help read

Suppose you are the system administrator in a school and want the new students to enter their first name and display it back. How do you do it? Here's the script:

#!/bin/bash

#This script reads the input and displays it

echo "Enter your Name, please:"

read YOURNAME

echo "Welcome to the new class, $YOURNAME"

Run the script after giving it the execute permission.

$ ./students.sh

Enter your Name, please:

Matt   #<-enter a name

Welcome to the new class, Matt

The input (what you typed) is the value of the variable **$YOUR-SELF** and the next line of code uses this variable. The double quotes do not interfere with the variable name **$YOURSELF**, and it expands to its value **Mark**.

There is another way of taking input from the user. This is by using read with **-p** option. The -p stands for prompt. So instead of using echo and then read, we can use read directly to ask for input.

Let us illustrate this with the following example; we will make changes in the file **students.sh** . Let us make a copy of the **studends.sh** and name it

$cat students1.sh

#!/bin/bash

#This script reads the input and displays it

read -p "Enter your name:" YOURNAME

echo "Welcome to the new class, $YOURNAME"

Run this script and see for yourself whether you get the same behavior.

Here's another example using the **read -p**, a simple additional table. Before dwelling into the script, let us learn about the **let** command.

You can use **help let** to find more information. The **let** command is used for arithmetical operations. The value of the variables are the operands. An operand is a number on which a mathematical equation is applied to. This is very simple. If **a** is the variable and we value it to **3**, then **3** is operand. Let us try to understand using one example:

```
$ a=100
$ b=200
$ let c=a+b
$ echo $c
300
```

Two variables are defined, **a** is valued to **100** and **b** to **200**. We use the **let** command to add the variable values and assign it to c. Instead of using let, you can use (( )).

```
$ n=5000
$ m=6000
$ ((o=n+m))
$ echo $o
11000
```

Please practice both the methods, before going to the following script.

```
#!/bin/bash
#The script adds values inputted by users

echo "Welcome to the Simple Addition table"

echo""

read -p "Enter your first number, please:" number1

echo""

read -p "Enter your second number, please:" number2

((number3=number1+number2))

echo "Your answer is $number3 "
```

Note: echo """ adds an empty line.

Try creating a multiplication table using the let command. You multiple using * (star).

CHAPTER 9 : INTRODUCING IF-THEN-ELSE-ELIF

The **if** statement is used for decision making, it is conditional. It decides two conditions, TRUE or FALSE and accordingly executes an appropriate code.

Before diving into **if-then-else** scripting, we need to cover the following topics:

- Positional Parameters
- Special Parameters

What are Positional Parameters?

The arguments that you input in the command line is the positional parameters. If you have a script, then it is the **$0** and then **$1** to **$n** .

Here is the content of batch script pos.sh . The \$0 the \ is used to invalidate the special meaning of **$**.

#!/bin/bash

echo "The Position \$0 is $0"
echo "This is Position \$1 $1 "
echo "This is Position \$2 $2 "
echo "This is Position \$3 $3 "

Let us execute the script to understand the positional parameters, with arguments Tom, Dick, and Harry

./pos.sh Tom Dick Harry

The Position $0 is ./pos.sh
This is Position $1 Tom
This is Position $2 Dick
This is Position $3 Harry

So it is now clear

$0 is the name of the script posh.sh

$1 is Tom

$2 is Dick

$3 is Harry

What are Special Parameters?

Now, let us understand Special Parameters, **$#** and **$@**, by incorporating them into the script, **pos.sh**, directly:

#!/bin/bash

echo "The Position \$0 is $0"

echo "This is Position \$1 $1 "

echo "This is Position \$2 $2 "

echo "This is Position \$3 $3 "

echo "The special parameter \$# is $# "

echo " The special parameter \$@ is $@"

After executing, you get the following output:

$ ./pos.sh Tom Dick Harry

The Position $0 is ./pos.sh

This is Position $1 Tom

This is Position $2 Dick

This is Position $3 Harry

The special parameter $# is 3

The special parameter $@ is Tom Dick Harry

Hence, **$#** counts the number of command-line arguments passed and **$@** merely stores the values passed in the command line in a list. There is another special parameter called **$*** which stores the values passed as arguments in a variable, it is, as you see, like **$@**. At this point, create few similar scripting before going to the next topic.

Understanding impact of echo in your script.

In this module, we study **echo**, how to insert a single line using ""
and a new line \n

This is a simple hello world script with no flourishes:

$ cat 1.sh
#!/bin/bash

echo "Hello World"

After running the script, note the prompts, lack of lines between
the adjoining prompts:

$ echo "Hello World"
Hello World
$

Inserting two empty lines using echo "" above and below the
statement echo "hello World" . Thus, you can change the appearance how your output appears in stdout.

Using **echo -e** and **\n** adds a carriage return. You have to use **echo**
-e with **\n** for new line. If you do not use echo with **-e** , the **\n** is
not effective, check the various examples and try yourself.

Using **\n** without with simple echo statement:

```
#!/bin/bash
echo  "Hello World\n"
```

Output: Note the appearance of \n - which obviously, you don't want to see.

```
$ sh 1.sh
Hello World\n
```

Code with -e:
```
#!/bin/bash
echo  -e "Hello World\n"
```

Output, notice the new line in the stdout.
```
$ sh 1.sh
Hello World

                #<- Insertion of a blank line, because -e option of
echo enables \n
$
```

There is one command that you should know that is used in Bash shell scripting. Unfortunately there is a prevailing tendency to suddenly introduce this command in shell scripts books/courses without first trying to explain what it does.

The **basename** command is used to strip a file of its preceding characters. For instance, suppose you have a file **test.sh** in your home directory. For that matter, any file will do. Put the absolute path of a file as a value to a variable like:

a=/home/bobbydeb/test.sh

Check the value of the variable:

$echo $a

/home/bobbydeb/test.sh

Now, apply the **basename** command on the file:

$ echo $a

/home/bobbydeb/test.sh

$ basename $a

test.sh

Various structures of if- then-else-elif

Structure 1:

if [test_expression]
then
      commands
fi

We study text expressions in the next topic.

Structure 2:

  if [test_expression]
  then
      commands
  else
      commands
  fi

Structure 3 :

```
if [ test_expression ]
then
        commands
elif [ test_expression ]
then
        commands

fi
```

Memorize these structure before going further!

Primary Expressions:

Primary expressions are the evaluation elements that are put inside the square brackets in the preceding examples. They are many primary examples and to list them all is beyond the scope of this book. However, you should try and use each expression in your scripts to learn the concepts. They are, but few things you need to master and if-then-else and looping structures are very important and acts as a basis to learn other scripting and pro-gramming languages.

[-b FILE]   True if a file exists and is a block file. A block file is associated with hard disk drives in Linux

[-c FILE]   True if a exists and is a character file.

[-d FILE]   True if a file exists and is a directory. In Linux everything is a file.

[-e FILE]   True if a exists.

[-f FILE]   True if a file exists and is a regular file.

Example with block expression. The block files are present in the **/dev** directory. The **/dev** stands for Device directory.

Go to /dev directory and do **ls -l**, here's a snippet of the long list:

we see three different types of files, autofs is a character file (note the c in the first bit), the block is a directory and dm-0 is a block file.

$ cd /dev

$ ls -l

total 0

crw-rw----. 1 root root   10, 57 Feb 25 14:21 autofs

drwxr-xr-x. 2 root root   640 Feb 25 14:20 block

brw-rw----. 1 root disk   253, 0 Feb 25 14:20 dm-0

Note: You need to be root to play around these files. Do not play on production servers at your office. Create your own Virtual server:

Create a file to check if **autofs** is a character file or not using if-then-else:

```
#!/bin/bash
if [ -c $1 ]
then
        echo " This is a character file"
else
        echo "This is not a character file"

fi
```

Note: It is recommended to put the variable in double quotes inside test statement. Otherwise, if any case the value of the variable becomes zero, then you end up with a syntax error.

Another primary expression not yet covered is **-s** . This tests whether a file has at least a byte written on it or not. System Administrators may use it to determine if the application logs have something written on them.

Create two files in your current directory using the touch command. You can call them **err1.log** and **err2.log**. In **err1.log**, write something using the **cat** command:

$ touch err1.log err2.log

bash-3.2$ cat > err1.log

Hello, this is not an empty file

Note: type **Control + C** to end writing in the file **err1.log**

Check if something is written in the files:

$ ls -l

total 8

-rw-r--r-- 1 bobbydeb bobbdydeb 30 May 10 18:22 err1.log

-rw-r--r-- 1 bobbydeb bobbydeb 0 May 10 18:16 err2.log

In this example, only **err1.log** has something written on it. Let's use this script to verify using **-s** expression.

$ cat errlog.sh

#!/bin/bash

if [-s $1]

   then

      echo " The file is not empty"

else

      echo " This file is empty"

fi

$ ./errlog.sh err1.log

The file is not empty

$ ./errlog.sh err2.log

This file is empty

You can also if the file is readable or not using **-r** and **! -r** expressions. The **!** is a negation and holds true if the file is not readable and the exit status is zero.

Again, create two files using the **touch** command

$ touch readme1.txt readme2.txt

Check using **ls -l** command if the files are created and also look carefully at the permissions:

-rw-r--r-- 1 bobbydeb bobbydeb 0 May 10 19:01 readme1.txt
-rw-r--r-- 1 bobbydeb bobbydeb 0 May 10 19:01 readme2.txt

Both the files have read permissions for the owner (bobbydeb), for the members of the group (bobbydeb) and for the rest of the world. Let's remove the READ permission for the owner for the file readme2.txt using the following command:

$chmod u-r readme2.txt

Again, do ls -l, there is no READ (r) permission for the file readme2.txt

--w-r--r-- 1 bobbydeb bobbydeb 0 May 10 19:01 readme2.txt

Let's create the script

$ cat readtester.sh

```
#!/bin/bash
if [ -r $1 ]
then
    echo "This file is readable"
else
echo  "This file is not readable"
fi
```

Check it against the files. Again $1 is the name of the file you must input:

$ ./readtester.sh readme1.txt
This file is readable
$ ./readtester.sh readme2.txt
This file is not readable

Let us modify the script to negate the -r expression using !

```
#!/bin/bash
if [ ! -r $1 ]
then
    echo "This file is readable"
else
echo "This file is not readable"
fi
```

Now check the file against the same files and compare the results:

```
$ ./readtester.sh readme1.txt
This file is not readable
$ ./readtester.sh readme2.txt
This file is readable
```

The results are the reverse of the previous script because adding the negation on **-r** has reversed the values. You must change the **echo** codes to make sense of this file now.

This is a new script for negating the read permission:

```
#!/bin/bash
if [ ! -r $1 ]
then
    echo "This file is not readable"
else
    echo "This file is readable"
fi
```

You have read about logical operators in earlier chapters, let's try to employ them in scripts in this section.

The operators are AND and OR. The AND operator is && while the OR operator is represented by !!.

Take two parameters -r and -f . The -r checks for the read permission and -f checks if the file exists. The AND operator succeeds if both the comparisons are TRUE.

Create a file called compare.txt.

$touch compare.txt

$ls -l

-rw-r--r-- 1 bobbydeb bobbydeb   0 May 10 19:10 compare.sh

This file exists (-f) is true and also it has read permission. The script looks like

$cat comp.sh

#!/bin/bash

if [[-f "$1" && -r "$1"]]

then

    echo "$1 file exists and is readable"

else

    echo "No such file exists"

fi

Notice, the usage of Double square brackets. If you cannot make the script run with single square brackets, use double. The [[ ]] is called Extended Test brackets.

Now, run the script against the compare.sh file, which exists and also has read permission.

The result is expected.

$ ./comp.sh compare.sh

compare.sh file exists and is readable

However, what if the run the script a file that exists but has no read permission. In this case, the test logic fails. The test logic returns FALSE and hence, the code after else statement executes.

Look at the following file:

--w-r--r-- 1 bobbydeb bobbydeb 0 May 10 19:01 readme2.txt

The file readme2.txt exists but has no READ permission for the owner. The && returns FALSE value :

$ ./comp.sh readme2.txt

No such file exists

This is because the echo statement is confusing. The file does exist but has no read permission and the AND logic goes FALSE.

You can make some modifications in the **comp.sh** file

#!/bin/bash

if [[-f "$1" || -r "$1"]]

then

    echo "$1 file exists but is not readable"

else

    echo "$1 File exists and is also readable"

fi

If you run the script against the file that has no read permission, the OR operator is useful because while -f is TRUE , -r is FALSE , which fulfills the demand of the OR operator.

$ ./comp.sh readme2.txt

readme2.txt file exists but is not readable

What happens if we run it against the file that exists and readable. The OR operator fails, and the code after else executes.

Using Test

Remember that [ ] is nothing but the **test** command and you can even write the same script in the following manner:

```
#!/bin/bash
if test -c $1
then
        echo " This is a character file"
else
        echo "This is not a character file"

fi
```

Note: $1 is the first parameter after the script name. We know that **autofs** is a character file. The prompt is hash #, because we logged in as root.

However, it is common practice to use [ ] . Rarely you would en-counter anyone using test instead of [ ] or [[ ]].

#./cdb.sh autofs

 # ./cdb.sh autofs
This is a character file

Let's check it against the block, which we know is a directory:

 # ./cdb.sh block
we get the following output.
This is not a character file

Thus, the script passes the logic state, it gives an output when TRUE and also when it is FALSE.

Create two script file for checking if $1 is a block or a directory.

At this point we take a detour and learn about integer operators of test:

Integer Operators used with test [ ]

The following comparison operators on integers returns Zero or TRUE when:

int1 -eq int2 : int1 is equal = to int2

int1 -ge int2 : int1 is greater or equal to >= int2

int2 -gt int2 : int1 is greater than > int2

int1 -le int2 : int1 is lesser than or equal <= to int2

int1 -lt int2 : int1 is lesser than < int2

int1 -ne int2 : int1 is not equal to int2

Check this example:

```
$ int1=500
$ int2=501
$ [ "int1" = "int2" ]
$ echo $?
1
```

Why is the exit status 1 ? Exit status other than zero means it is an Error. It is error because we have used test or [ ] to compare int1 and int2 and check if they are equal. They are not. Hence the error. But we can still make the value zero or TRUE by not even changing the values. This is possible by using ! in front of =.

It negates the equality, and it reads "Test if int1 and int2 are not equal". If they are not equal, the exit status is ZERO or TRUE.

```
$ int1=500
$ int2=50000
$ [ "int1" != "int2" ]
$ echo $?
0
```

The exit value 0 means the command is successful.

Another example using the = string operator

```
#!/bin/bash

if [ $1 = "peter" ]
        then
        echo " Let's go to the movie."
else
        echo " Bye Bye "
fi
```

In this example, you need to put the name peter as the first argument after the script name. $1 is the first argument and is compared to the string peter. If the comparison succeeds, then you see the "Let's go to the movie" phrase, if you put another name, you see "Bye Bye" as the output.

$ ./movie.sh peter

Let's go to the movie

$ ./movie.sh bobby

Bye Bye

For mathematical/arithmetic comparisons it is not necessary to use either single or square brackets, you can also use round brackets. This is a favorite Interview question as well. Look at the following example, that employs round brackets and two positional parameters:

```bash
#!/bin/bash

x=$1
y=$2

if (( x > y ))
then
      echo "Yes, X is greater"
else
      echo "Something is burning"
fi
```

$ ./maths.sh 89 900

Something is burning

$ ./maths.sh 999 777

Yes, X is greater

Note: There are no double quotes in the variables, it is allowed when using round brackets. You would, most likely, get a syntax error if you use single square brackets.

In the following example has two logic decisions, anyone less than 5 years old is not charged any fee, while any child above 6 is charged 50 dollars. Create more scripts in the same vein using Integer operators.

```
#!/bin/bash

echo ""
echo " Welcome to the Carnival"
echo ""
echo "Enter your age to know your fee"

read -p "Enter your age:" age

if [ $age -le 5 ]
then
      echo "You have to pay NO FEES"
elif [ $age -ge 6 ]
then
      echo " You have to pay 50 dollars"
fi
```

Tip: Make it is a point to use [[instead of [. Double [[has several enhancements over single [. In this book, both the types of brackets are used.

CHAPTER 10 : LOOKING AT LOOPING

Looping is an action that starts and repeatedly restarts until a condition is met. Computers are very good at repetitive tasks. It is the reason why we use loops.

The FOR-loop syntax is easy:

for <variable> in <list>

do

  <some_action>

done

The variable loops thru the values specified in the list. For example, if we want to echo the countdown to a rocket launch from 5 to 0 , we can use the syntax to write the script as follows:

#!/bin/bash

#The countdown to a rocket launch from 5 to 0

for c in 5 4 3 2 1 0

do

  echo $c

done

The expected output is

5

4

3

2

1

0

Yes, it is as simple as that. The variable **c** is given the first value in the list, which, in this case is **5** and <some_action> is performed which is to **echo** the value of **c**. This goes on till the end of the value in the list 0 (zero).

Thus, the components of the script are:

c which is the variable and gets to act on each value of the list.

5 4 3 2 1 0 is the list

do

echo $c Action is to DO echo $c

Let's take this opportunity to combine decision making (if then else) with "for" looping. We will enhance the same script and decide not to echo any value greater 2.

Check the enhanced script:

```
#!/bin/bash
#The countdown to rocket launch from 5 to 0
for c in 5 4 3 2 1 0
do
   if [[ $c < 2 ]]
then
echo $c
fi
done
```

The script echoes only those items in the list which are less than 2 . Mind it, if it is less than 2, hence only 1 and 0 is echoed back to the screen.

Let's look at a tougher example using backticks. As we know, backticks are used in command substitutions, any command inside the backticks is evaluated by the shell.

For a practical usage, you can assign commands inside a backticks and its output as value for a variable.

Check this sequence of commands:

$ ls

Expected output

countdown.sh first.py freetxt.sh freetxt.txt

Now to assign the output of ls command to a variable, let's say VALUE , we enter the following commands

$VALUE=`ls`

$echo $VALUE

Let us use the "for" loop to display the content of all text files in a directory one by one. Here a variable TEXTFILES is defined. Its value is the output of the command ls *.txt, which shows all the files with .txt extension. A temporary variable works on the value of TEXTFILE thru the cat $text which displays the content of each txt file found in the current directory.

```
#!/bin/bash
#Displaying the contents of all text files in the current direc-
tory.

TEXTFILES='ls *.txt'

for text in "$TEXTFILES"
do
  SHOWFILES="`cat $text`"
  echo $SHOWFILES
```

done

In the real-world, the for loops is synonymous with counter mechanism in BASH. You can affect counting or incrementing and decrementing by the following syntaxes:

$i=$((i++)) #Adds One to the variable 1 and then used it a loop to increment. Note the double brackets to enable arithmetic expression.

Or

counter=`expr $counter + 1`

CHAPTER 11:
DETOUR TO SED

The most important **sed** usage is in substitution, let's consider the following text, you can call ancients.txt

The Ancients under the names of Apophthegms_, comprehended what we

call wise Sayings, generous and noble Sentiments, Jests and witty

Repartees: However, according to our Notions, the Apophthegm thus

differs from a Jest or Repartee, that the first is generally Grave and Instructive; whereas Jests and Repartees instruct us and make

us merry at once; nay, sometimes these are merely diverting, and

sometimes sharp and Satirical.

Let us replace "the" with capital version THE. Not sed is case sensitive and hence, won't act on The (title case). It uses "s" command to actuate the substation and it has been enclosed in single quotes, because what's inside contains special characters which may be wrongly interpreted by the shell.

$ sed 's/the/THE/' ancients.txt

The ancients under THE names of _Apophthegms_, compre-

hended what we

call wise Sayings, generous and noble Sentiments, Jests and witty

Repartees: However, according to our Notions, THE Apophthegm thus

differs from a Jest or Repartee, that THE first is generally Grave and Instructive; whereas Jests and Repartees instruct us and make

us merry at once; nay, sometimes THEse are merely diverting, and

sometimes sharp and Satirical.

The sed command does not alter the original file which remains the same, you can redirect the output to a different file by using the following command:

$sed 's/the/THE/' ancients.txt > ancients_new.txt

Precautions while using sed:

1) Special characters like white space , ' should be escaped using \

2) There is no need to use quotes if there are no special characters.

For example, the following command is valid.

$sed s/the/THE/ ancients.txt

3) What if you want to add a space between each character in THE , like T H E.

$sed s/the/T H E/ ancients.txt

You get the following error message

sed: -e expression #1, char 7: unterminated `s' command

Try enclosing them in single quotes, this time it works. Use double quotes as well and see what happens. But we can even make the example without quotes work by using the following example. Here the two white spaces are escaped by the \

$sed s/the/T\H\E/ ancients.txt

Now, consider the following text:

The fox had a pal called The tiger
The tiger had a pal called a lion. The lion was mean

Use the nearly same example previously used to replace The with THE

$ sed 's/The/THE/' the.txt
THE fox had a pal called The tiger

THE tiger had a pal called a lion. The lion was mean

Note: the.txt is the name of the file and though you don't need to use quotes, do use it as a good practice whether you have special characters or not.

Only the first occurrences of The were changed to THE. To apply it globally, you must use the **g (global) modifier** to make sure that the substitution is global.

$sed 's/The/THE/g' the.txt

The result that you get by using **g** is as follows:

THE fox had a pal called THE tiger
THE tiger had a pal called a lion. THE lion was mean

Note: You can use any delimiter apart from / in sed, it can even be a comma, hence the following example is also valid. Using the the.txt, let's replace fox with a dog and use comma as the delimiter.

$ sed 's,fox,dog,' the.txt
The dog had a pal called The tiger

The tiger had a pal called a lion. The lion was mean

Using Regular expression in sed

Regular expressions are a hard concept to understand. You need lots of practice and patience.

Matching a single character using wild expression dot ".". The quotes have no meaning here.

$ cat dot.txt
Cat are not very friendly. I used to hate cats but now I like cats. I have a cat called Kitty.

$ sed 's/c.t/mat/g' dot.txt
Cat are not very friendly. I used to hate mats but now I like mats. I have a mat called Kitty.

Check how, the word Cat was ignored because it starts with capital C.

#Pattern matching at the end and the beginning of the line.

While it seems easy, it is confusing as well. So, don't take this for granted. Use the example below:

$ cat matching.txt

First line

Second line differs from the line First

Third line differs from the line Second

Suppose you want to replace the Fir of first with **Thir** but limit it to when it appears at the beginning of the line use ^ (the symbol above the number 6 on your keyboard). The idea is to ignore the First in the second line which occurs at the end of the line.

$ sed 's/^Fir/Thir/' matching.txt

The output is

Thirst line

Second line differs from the line First

Third line differs from the line Second

Now, change the First in the second line:

$ sed 's/$First/Thir/' matching.txt

The output is

First line

Second line differs from the line First

Third line differs from the line Second

But, as you nothing has changed. The reason is the placement of the $, it should be after First as shown in the following example:

$ sed 's/First$/ST/' matching.txt

First line

Second line differs from the line ST

Third line differs from the line Second

Note: Do no copy and paste content from this book right onto the console. Please type the text. Quotes are treated differently in various word processing software. Also, results may vary per operating System.

Try similar exercise with the word Second. If you do not practice, you soon forget everything.

Using square brackets to match a single character:

Here is the file to test for testing [ ] bracket range. Anything in the square bracket will match only a single character

[123] will match either 1 or 2 or 3. It won't match 12 or 23.

[1-100] will match any single number between 1 and 100.

[a-zA-Z] will match a single character between lower/upper class a and z.

Let's work on the word day to illustrate the examples.

$ cat single.txt

Today was the first Day of school.

The first day is always exciting.

I wish my brother was here.

Notice that the content has day spelt in lower and title case, to change it to fully upper case, you use the following sed regular expression and modifiers.

$ sed 's/[Dd]ay/DAY/g' single.txt

ToDAY was the first DAY of school.

The first DAY is always exciting.

I wish my brother was here.

More sed modifiers
Consider the file below:

$ cat lines.txt

This the first line

The second line

The third line

You can use a simple sed script to change the lower case the to upper case THE using

sed 's/the/THE/' lines.txt

When you use the modifier -n , it prevents the printing of any anything on the standard output unless explicitly specified.

$ sed -n 's/the/THE/' lines.txt

$

As you can see in the last example, there is no output. You have to use it with -p modifier. With the -p modifier, the standard output shows only the lines the modified. Know the difference.

$ sed -n 's/the/THE/p' lines.txt

This THE first line

In the last example, you can see unchanged lines, i.e., the second and the third lines are NOT printed.

If you want to have more than one substitutions to occur from a single sed command, then use the -e modifier in the following way:

$sed -e 's/This/THIS/' -e 's/second/SECOND/' lines.txt

THIS the first line

The SECOND line

The third line

CHAPTER 12:
WORKING WITH CASE
CONDITIONALS

Case statements provide a shorter way to check a "value" against a "series of values". The "series of values are search" patterns tested against the "value". If there is a match, then case allows execution of a block of code.

Here, is the syntax of the case statement program, the **$some_variable_value** is a variable and its value is matched against "**some_pattern**". If there is a match, "**Code_to_run**" is executed.

```
case $some_variable_value in
        " some_pattern")
        Code_to_run
        ;;
        " ")
        ;;
esac
```

Now, consider a small example. Linux/Ubuntu Operating systems have multiple run levels. The run levels are the modes on which your system runs. They are normally 6 run levels. For example run level 0 (zero) signifies halt, run levels 3 and 5 are generally the run levels you would be working on. Run level 1 is when you need the system for performing system administration work. To find the run level you are in, you use the commands **runlevel** or **who -r** . Let's us create a script that identifies whether you are in the desired run level of 5. While the script may not have significant usage, it will help you understand how case scripts work.

A variable called **levels** is defined in the script. The value of which is the command **who -r** and to which **awk** has been applied to get the value of the second field.

$who -r

run-level 5 2017-04-15 22:24

As you can see, the second field is 5 which is the run level the system is currently on. Using awk, we extract the second field and use it for a set of patterns to check the variable levels.

Here's the script

$cat level.check
#!/bin/bash

#This script checks levels on which your System is running on

levels=$(who -r | awk '{print $2}')

case $levels in
  "5")
  echo " Your System in running on level 5"
  ;;
  *)
  echo "Your system is not running on level 5"
esac

The script should read like, check the value of levels (which we know is 5) against the pattern
"5")
If it matches, then the block of code

echo " Your System in running on level 5"

is executed.

If the value of who -r is anything other than 5, let's say 3, the catch-it-all , the dust-bin of sorts.

*)

Is matched and the code is

echo "Your system is not running on level 5"

is executed and the script exists. This is in case, the pattern is 5 is not matching with the value of the variables levels.

However, the main usage of case conditionals is in menus. Let's go ahead and create one.

Heere is a nifty little script that determines if your system has 32 or 64 architecture. Here's the script:

```
$./archChecker.sh
You have a 32 bit Operating System
$cat archChecker.sh
#!/bin/bash

#This script checks the architecture of your system

arch=$(uname -a | awk '{print $14}')

case $arch in
    "i386")
    echo " You have a 32 bit Operating System"
    ;;
    "x86_64")
    echo " You have a 64 bit Operating System"
    ;;
    *)
    echo "Makes no sense"
    ;;
esac
```

Run the script after giving it the execute permission:

```
$./archChecker.sh
You have a 32 bit Operating System
```

Let's write a small menu based script using the case conditionals. Here's a birthday script that you can make for your office administrator:

```
#!/bin/bash

#Birthday Finder

echo "       Birthday of your co-worker"
echo "                 WELCOME"
echo " ************************************"
echo " Choose the initial of your co-worker"
echo
echo
echo " [J]ames, Smith"
echo " [M]aria, Claires"
echo " [T]om, Alters"
echo " [B]obby, Deb"
echo

echo "Enter the Initial of your coworker:"
read coworker

case $coworker in
       "J" | "j" )
       echo " James' birthday is on 1st March"
```

```
;;
"M" | "m")
echo " Maria's birthday is on 25th March"
;;
"T" | "t")
echo "Tom's birthday is on 15th April"
;;
"B" | "b")
echo "Bobby's birth is on 2nd June"
;;
*)
echo "Wrong Input, enter the correct Initial"
;;

esac
```

When you run the script, you will get the following output:

```
$./birthday.sh
        Birthday of your co-worker
              WELCOME
************************************
Choose the initial of your co-worker


[J]ames, Smith
[M]aria, Claires
[T]om, Alters
```

LEARNING BASH SHELL SCRIPTING GENTLY

[B]obby, Deb

Enter the Initial of your coworker:

#At this point enter the initial of your co-worker, suppose you enter b or B

b

Bobby's birth is on 2nd June

$

Argument Identifier

There is a shell script construct that determines whether you have passed any argument on the command line script that you are running. You have learned about **$#** earlier in the book; it is a special parameter that counts the number of arguments passed on the command line. You find other constructs doing the same thing online, but this is the simplest.

$ cat argument_tester.sh

#!/bin/bash

if ["$#" -ne 1]

then

      echo "Usage: Please pass an argument for $0 script to work "

fi

If you run the script without providing any argument to the script it displays the message after echo, $0 echo esthe argument

101

ZERO which is the script name. While if you pass any other argument, the script will "seem" to execute silently.

First, without any argument:

$ ./argument_tester.sh

You get

Usage: Please pass an argument for ./argument_tester.sh script to work

Secondly, without any argument:

$ ./argument_tester.sh 5

$

Seems to execute silently.

The construct is mostly used as an adjunct to other scripts; however, you need to be careful what the requirement of other scripts is. It is necessary to look for a number, say 5 used in the previous example; it could be a word or an alphabetical character, so you must pass the correct exit status to the rest of the script. To do that, use exit 1 as the status confirming the exit of the script when no argument is returned. So, the, this script looks like

#!/bin/bash

if ["$#" -ne 1]

then

    echo "Usage: Please pass an argument for $0 script to work "

      exit 1

fi

You can create a script that translates numbers to digits. That is, if you enter one as an argument, the script translates to its number equivalent. You should use the construct we have learned to ensure that some argument is passed to the script without which the script exits with an error status.

```bash
#!/bin/bash
#This will check if an argument is passed, otherwise will exit with an
# error status.
if [ "$#" -ne 1 ]
then
        echo "Usage: Please pass an argument for $0 script to work "
        exit 1
fi

case "$1" in
    one)
    echo " The translated numerical is 1"
    ;;
    two)
    echo " The translated numerical is 2 "
    ;;
    three)
    echo " The translated numerical is 3"
    ;;
esac
```

First Test, without an argument

./magic.sh

Usage: Please pass an argument for ./magic.sh script to work

Second Test, with arguments

$ ./magic.sh one

The translated numerical is 1

$ ./magic.sh two

The translated numerical is 2

$ ./magic.sh three

The translated numerical is 3

However, some quality related questions arise, which are follows:

1) What happens if the argument is in title or Capital case? Like One or ONE
2) What happens if the argument is other than one, two or three?

You can try and modify the script to solve the quality questions:

```bash
#!/bin/bash
#This will check if an argument is passed, otherwise will exit with an
# error status.
if [ "$#" -ne 1 ]
then
        echo "Usage: Please pass an argument for $0 script to work "
            exit 1
fi

case "$1" in
        [oO][nN][eE])
        echo " The translated numerical is 1"
        ;;
        [tT][wW][oO])
        echo " The translated numerical is 2 "
        ;;
        [tT][hH][rR][eE][eE])
        echo " The translated numerical is 3"
        ;;
esac
```

For anything other than one, two or three, you can add what you have learned earlier, that is,

```bash
*)
        echo "No other argument apart from one, two, three accepted"
```

;;

In the English language, there are five vowels a, e, i, o, u. Let's create a script that not only exits if there is no argument passed to the script but also exits if there is more than one character in the script. The name of the script is vowels.sh

```
#!/bin/bash
#The following part of the script will check if an argument is passed,
# otherwise will exit with an error status.
if [ "$#" -ne 1 ]
then
        echo "Usage: Please pass an argument for $0 script to work "
        exit 1
fi
#The following part of the script will check exit if the first argument is more than
#one character
#Define a variable called input which is equal to the first argument
input="$1"
```

#Define a variable check which will run a command wc command and test #if the number of characters is more than 1

check=$(echo "$input" | wc -c)

if ["$check" -ne 2]

then

      echo " You can enter ONLY one letter"

      exit 1

fi

case "$1" in

    [aA]|[eE]|iI]|[oO]|[uU])

      echo "Yes, ***$1*** is a VOWEL"

    ;;

    *)

      echo "***$1*** is not a vowel"

esac

Some notes about the script vowels.sh

The following part of the script should ideally check for being not equal to 1 rather than 2. The reason it is **two** is because **wc -c** command adds an invisible newline character.

check=$(echo "$input" | wc -c)

if ["$check" -ne 2]

then

      echo " You can enter ONLY one letter"

      exit 1

fi

It can be illustrated with an example

$ char=a

$ echo $char | wc -c

2

You get into these kinds of surprises every day. You just have to learn!

CHAPTER 13: LOOPS AGAIN

It is my observation that learners tend to forget what they have learned quickly unless the topics are constantly revisited. Some of us may have already forgotten loops after going through the case conditionals. Hence, the endeavor is to revisit the subject of looping again, this time going bit advanced. Let's start with a simple example as shown:

#!/bin/bash

#In this script the variable fruits is looped through various names of fruits with the help of the code that #starts with echo

#Notice how the variable fruits is treated with a preceding dollar #sign.

for fruits in apple orange kiwi banana mango; do

echo "My favorite fruit is $fruits "

done

Expected result:

$./fruits.sh

My favorite fruit is apple

My favorite fruit is orange

My favorite fruit is kiwi

My favorite fruit is banana

My favorite fruit is mango

Instead of typing the names of the values the variable has to loop through, you can use command outputs enclosed in backticks. For example, see how the find command that finds the names of the files in the current directory (the dot is the current directory), while the type is f in the following find command:

$ find . -type f

The script will look like:

```
#!/bin/bash
for files in `find . -type f` ; do
echo "The name of the file is $files "
done
```

Expected output is

$ ./files.sh

The name of the file is ./fruits.sh

The name of the file is ./students1.sh

The name of the file is ./addtab.sh

The name of the file is ./filetypes.sh

The name of the file is ./tn1

The name of the file is ./bin/add.sh

The name of the file is ./bin/calc.sh

The name of the file is ./bin/simple_script.sh

The name of the file is ./bin/minus.sh

The name of the file is ./bin/1

The name of the file is ./bin/postions.sh

The name of the file is ./pos.sh

The name of the file is ./hello

There is another aspect of for looping, taking values from the command line as opposed to putting values in the script.

For loop example inside a script:

Content of counter.sh file

#!/bin/bash

for variable in 1, 2, 3, 4 ,5 ; do

<code>

done

Now, specify the values in the command line. Here's how:

$./counter.sh 1 2 3 4 5

The content of **counter.sh** does not have an "in" included. The script now looks like:

#!/bin/bash

for variable; do

echo $variable

done

Note: There is no "in" provided.

However, you must run the script with arguments to get the following output:

```
$ ./counter.sh 1 2 3 4 5
1
2
3
4
5
```

Let's create a script that that counts the number of words of text files. The text files are names of the files given as $1, $2, $3 arguments in the command line. We loop to check each file for the number of words they contain.

Here is the file called words.sh:

```
#!/bin/bash

for file ; do
        echo `wc -w $file`
done
```

You run it like

$./words.sh lsbChecker test1

The output you get is

43 lsbChecker

0 test1

Here, lsbChecker and test1 are $1 and $2 positional parameters. Moreover, the **wc -w** command counts the number of words in each file.

You can now learn about **while** and **until** loops. At the very beginning, you must try to understand the difference between the two. These looping mechanisms are notoriously confusing. Feel free to take time to understand the underlying context.

You have learned about the $@ stores the values passed in the command line in a list. You can incorporate it in the for loops to display all the arguments passed on the command line after the script name. You can use it with $# which counts the number of arguments passed.

```
$ cat arg_counter.sh
#!/bin/bash
echo "The number of arguments is ***$#****"
for argu in $@
do
        echo $argu
done
```

Output:

```
$ ./arg_counter.sh 1 39 48 48 40 a b 8 30 30
The number of arguments is ***10****
1
39
48
48
40
a
b
8
30
30
```

The simplistic approach of other for-loop examples is not sufficient; the following syntax redefines the usage of for-loop, it is an advanced form of for-loop used in real-word.

for keyword **((control expressions))**

followed by

do

　　a command or multiple commands

done

The control expression starts with a variable and a value followed by a limit mechanism that stops the looping, and a counting condition for the loop variable to reach the termination.

Control expressions are separated by semi-colons.

x=1, variable and a value

x <= 10 , the loop will terminate when the value is 10

x++, the counter incrementor

#!/bin/bash

for ((x=1; x <= 10; x++))

do

　　echo $x

done

The While and Until loops.

Like the if-then-else decision making, the while loop checks for a condition "while" the condition is true. The until loop checks if the condition is false until it becomes true when it stops executing the code. Which means that the until loops continue executing until a condition becomes true. For instance, if x variable is valued to 500, then you can employ the until loop to check numbers, say 1 to 499 till it gets to the number 500 and the until loop terminates. So that narrow downs the situations where you employ the until loop. You employ **until** loop in situations where you have at least 1 false condition to evaluate to run the loop at least once. Likewise, you employ while loop in situations where you have at least 1 TRUE condition to begin with.

However, what is the difference between while and for loops? In for loops, the number of iterations is known, in while loop, this is not the case. The number of iterations is not known and is only subject to the while loop's condition becoming false – that is when the loop terminates. Of course, you may use while loop even if you know the number of iterations, but why write more code when you can easily use the for-loop.

The <code> between the do and done keeps on executing till the condition is true.

while [condition is true]

do

<code>

done

The <code> between the do and done keep on executing till the condition is false.

until [condition is false]

do

<code>

done

While loop examples

In this example, the execution of the script depends upon the input. If the number of leaves is more than 5, it renders the condition of the while loop false and the script immediately terminates. However, if your input is less than 5, the loop becomes infinite.

#!/bin/bash

echo " Enter the number of times you missed school in a month"

read LEAVE

while [$LEAVE -le 5]

do

echo "Your Leaves are under control"

done

Note: Add exit 0 after the echo statement to prevent the script from going to the infinite loop

Look at the following example:

```
#!/bin/bash

x=500

while [ "$x" -ne 400 ]
do
        echo $x

done
```

The script fulfills the condition, x is valued to 500 and is asked to test that it is not equal to 400 which is true, and then code block has to echo the value of x variable which is 500. Execute the script, and you find that while just cannot stop executing the code. To stop the execution of the code, you must add exit 0 at the end of the script. What it means is that once while tests that the condition is True it should exit the script with the help of exit 0. The correct script looks like:

```
#!/bin/bash

x=500

while [ "$x" -ne 400 ]
do
        echo $x
exit 0
done
```

Now, the script only echoes the value of X ONCE and exit script. Otherwise, the script goes into an infinite loop.

In the real world, the while loop scripts are used with shift. The shift command shifts arguments from right to left.

You can again use the special variable $# that counts the number of arguments passed after $0 (that is the name of the script). So, whatever argument you enter in the command line is acted upon while $# is not equal to zero. Why "not equal" to zero? Because you have to put the argument and while condition only acts if the condition is true.

Let's construct the script step by step:

$ cat do.sh

#!/bin/bash

while ["$#" -ne 0]

do

> **echo "$1"**

> **exit 0**

done

The while condition is True because the argument has 1 argument, and the up to the first parameter 9.

$ ./do.sh 9

$ 9

What if you add more arguments?

$ ./do.sh 9 8 7 6

We still get the same output 9, what we need to do is shift the $2 (here it is 8) to $1 position, and so on, this is done by using the **shift** command.

```
#!/bin/bash
while [ "$#" -ne 0 ]
do
        echo "$1"
        shift
done
```

Alternately, of course, you may choose not use shift and in this case, use $@ without shift will, nearly, serve the same purpose.

```
#!/bin/bash
while [ "$#" -ne 0 ]
do
        echo "$@"
        exit 0
done
```

However, the output appears in the single line. Remember the meaning of $@ which is that it merely stores the values passed in the command line in a LIST.

A common use of while loop is with the read command. You can use it to read the system files and display them as shown in the following example and script

LEARNING BASH SHELL SCRIPTING GENTLY

The **/etc/hosts** files is a sort of early DNS (Domain Naming System) and keep the database of IP address to hostname translation of your system. In the script, the content of the **hosts** file is read into the variable "hosts" which echoes back after 1 second using the **sleep 1** command. Since hosts file contains several lines each line is echoed until the end of the line is reached which returns a Non-Zero exit value compromising the while procedure which can only run when the exit value is 0 or TRUE.

```
#!/bin/bash
while read hosts
do
      echo $hosts
      sleep 1
done < /etc/hosts
```

Note: Reading the file in "done" may seem odd. However, consider the block of code as a single command.

The expected output is the following lines appearing after 1 second:

```
$ ./hosts.sh
127.0.0.1 localhost
127.0.1.1 linux1978
```

The following lines are desirable for IPv6 capable hosts
::1 ip6-localhost ip6-loopback
fe00::0 ip6-localnet
ff00::0 ip6-mcastprefix
ff02::1 ip6-allnodes
ff02::2 ip6-allrouters

Until loop examples

If you were to vocalize what until-loop does, then you can say to yourself that until the condition becomes true, the looping continues. Alternatively, when false it continues, when true it terminates.

```bash
#!/bin/bash
until [[ $guess =  25 ]]
do
        echo "Guess a number between 0 - 25"
        read guess
        echo "$guess"
done
```

When the script is run without the double brackets in the condition, **$guess = 25**, you get an error like

./guess.sh: line 3: [: =: unary operator expected

Hence, double brackets were used, which supports more advanced features.

Check another example of **until loop**:

Notice the use of single brackets as opposed to the double brackets in the previous example, in this example, the read command got the numerical value before the until loop condition comes to picture, hence, single brackets is used on the condition.

```
#!/bin/bash

echo "Welcome to the rocket launcher reverse countdown,
input your start number"
read STARTNUMBER

until [ $STARTNUMBER -eq 0 ]
do
        echo "Launch Count starts - $STARTNUMBER"
        STARTNUMBER="`expr $STARTNUMBER - 1`"
        sleep 1

done

echo " The Rocket is  LAUNCHING"
```

The **echo** command takes the input from you and the **read** command stores it in the variable STARTNUMBER. The variable is tested against the value of 0, so until STARTNUMBER becomes zero using mathematical expression it keeps on executing the code. The sleep command waits for 1 second to add little drama to the script. Check the mathematical expression valued to the STARTNUMBER in backticks.

$./reverserocketcount.sh

Welcome to the rocket launcher reverse countdown, input your start number

10

Launch Count starts - 10

Launch Count starts - 9

Launch Count starts - 8

Launch Count starts - 7

Launch Count starts - 6

Launch Count starts - 5

Launch Count starts - 4

Launch Count starts - 3

Launch Count starts - 2

Launch Count starts - 1

The Rocket is LAUNCHING

Let's modify the previous script for the while loop. Remember, the while loop will execute only when the condition is true, once it becomes false, it will stop executing.

```
#!/bin/bash

STARTNUMBER=10


while [ $STARTNUMBER -ge 0 ]
do
      echo "Launch Count starts - $STARTNUMBER"
      STARTNUMBER="`expr $STARTNUMBER - 1`"
      sleep 1

done

echo " The Rocket is  LAUNCHING"
```

This script is not asking input from the command line, the reverse counting starting from 10 is hard coded, with variable STARTNUMBER=10. Now, you know that while loop condition must be true so that it can execute. The condition here is that STARTNUMBER value, which is 10, is indeed greater than 0

while [$STARTNUMBER -ge 0]

Hence, the first condition is met. The logic must be built in such a way so that the code stops executing when the condition becomes false. How does the condition become false? The expression

STARTNUMBER="`expr $STARTNUMBER - 1`"

Keeps on reducing the STARTNUMBER's value, 10, with minus 1. This is in a loop and when STARTNUMBER becomes minus 1 or – 1 , the condition while [$STARTNUMBER -ge 0]

becomes FALSE and the script stops executing.

$./reverserocketcount.sh

Launch Count starts - 10

Launch Count starts - 9

Launch Count starts - 8

Launch Count starts - 7

Launch Count starts - 6

Launch Count starts - 5

Launch Count starts - 4

Launch Count starts - 3

Launch Count starts - 2

Launch Count starts - 1

Launch Count starts - 0

Since until loop works on the premise that is False to start with. The script using until will continue executing until the event become True.

Break and Continue

The break and continue commands are used in loops to disrupt the normal functioning of the script. Before you learn about **break** and **continue** commands, let's take our, by now, usual detour and learn about the date command. These commands are very important in system administration because they are used to run scripts in future dates or timestamp back up files.

Run the date command:

$date

Mon Apr 24 00:11:22 IST 2017

If you want to see the day of the week only, enter:

$date +%a

Mon

To see the date only:

$date %d

24

To see the month only:

$date +%b

Apr

To display only the Minute

$date +%M

14

As you can see they are innumerable uses of the **date** command!

Break command is used in looping to break the flow of the script. Let's start with a simple for-loop script that displays the Alphabets your kid has learned. Here "**a**" is the variable that loops through the values hardcoded in the script, A B C D E F G H, the code between "do" and "done" just echoes the value of variable "**a**" for each value.

#!/bin/bash

for a in A B C D E F G H
do
> **echo "I learnt $a "**
done

The expected output is :

I learned A

I learned B

I learned C

I learned D

I learned E

I learned F

I learned G

I learned H

Imagine, let's apply the **break** command, for instance, you kid need not learn anything on Sunday. You know that the **date** command has an option to display only the day, which is

$date +%a
Mon

So, let's add a code that disables the running of the code because it is Sunday, - a holiday for kids using the if statement. Understand the main purpose of **break**. The purpose of break is NOT to allow execution of the block of code that is below it. In this example, the brea does not allow the execution of the code based on the day of the week. Had it been Monday or any day barring Sunday, the break command does not hinder the execution of

echo "I learned $a "

```
#!/bin/bash

for a in A B C D E F G H
do
if [ `date +%a` = "Sun" ]
    then
    echo " Today is Sunday, and I will not study."
    fi
    break
    echo "I learned $a "
done
```

Expected output:

Today is Sunday, and I will not study

Don't get confused by the usage of backticks to run the date command.

You can use

$(date +%a)

Or

Put it in another variable and then do the conditional test.

So even this variant works:

```
#!/bin/bash

for a in A B C D E F G H
do
if [ $(date +%a) = "Sun" ]
    then
    echo " Today is Sunday, and I will not study."
    fi
    break

    echo "I learned $a "
done
```

So, does this variant, in which "dow" is defined as the variable whose value will be the output of the command **date +%a**

```
#!/bin/bash

for an in A B C D E F G H
do
dow=$(date +%a)

if [ $dow = "Sun" ]
    then
    echo " Today is Sunday, and I will not study."
    fi
    break

    echo "I learned $a "
done
```

In the real world, the break is often used to exit from an infinite loop. You can create an infinite loop by using two commands true and false. If you want more information on true, enter the following command.

$ info true

It does nothing apart from returning a TRUE or zero value. Similarly, the false command returns a non-true value. They are used for testing in the real world.

```
#/bin/bash
while true
do
        echo `ls -l`
done
```

Note: You can use : (colon) to represent true. It is a common interview question. It is also called null.

If you run the script, your whole screen is a mess, and as the script runs **ls -l** , you have to use **control + c** to exit. It is an example of an infinite loop.

Continue loop

The **continue** loop is used to miss a current iteration and go to the next iteration:

```
$ cat cont.sh
#!/bin/bash
for x in 1 2 3 4 5
do
        if [[ x = 4 ]]
        then
        echo "Skipping the Fourth Iteration"
        continue
        fi
echo $x

done
```

The result that you get is as follows:

$ ./cont.sh

1

2

3

Skipping the Fourth Iteration

5

You must understand every part of the script; it is a precursor to understanding nested loops. The main component of the script is that it loops 5 times. The **echo $x** SHOULD display 1,2,3,4,5 (if it were not for the decision "if statement") in a loop, but we have set a condition, the condition is that on the 4th loop, that is, when x = 4, the loop encounters the **continue** command. The continue command does not allow the execution of **echo $x** only when **x = 4**.

CHAPTER 14: INTRODUCING FUNCTIONS

An application may need to act many times. For instance, consider a client application that must poll its server repeatedly over a period for security reasons. So, there is a need for a reusable piece of code in the script that recalls this component or piece of code. The reusable code is called the function.

The syntax of a function is universal. That is, most programming and scripting languages have the same syntax:

new_function ()

{

Some code

}

Earlier, you learned about true which does nothing but return a true value. You can use your first function in a script using the true command.

#!/bin/bash

new_function()

{

true

}

As expected, it returns zero, which you check using echo **$?** . It is an example where you have defined the function. However, the main purpose of a function is that it should is called within the script or the program.

How do we call a function within the script?

#!/bin/bash

function_hello()

{

echo "hello from a Function"

}

function_hello

The script is divided into two portions, and this order must be followed. First, define a function and then only call it. Otherwise, your script will fail.

Step 1: Defining a function

function_hello()

{

```
echo "hello  from a Function."

}
```

Step 2: Calling a function

function_hello

And, then executing the script. It is important to note that you have to define a function first and then call it. Bash scripts work sequentially from top to bottom. You can define multiple functions and call them as many times you want. There is no order for calling functions once you have them defined.

In the following script, two functions are first defined and then called. Notice after defining the functions, you need not bother about the order of the functions you call in your script.

LEARNING BASH SHELL SCRIPTING GENTLY

```
#!/bin/bash

#Define functions

func1()
{
    echo "Hello This is Function1"
}

func2()
{
    echo "Hello This is Function2"
}

#calling the functions

echo "calling the functions"

sleep 2
func1
sleep 2
func2
sleep 2
func1
sleep 2
func2
```

Functions invariably work with variables. They are two kinds of variables in scripts that have function calls. The globally defined variable and a variable that is within a script. The global variables, of course, can be called at any point in the script and is put in place before you define a function. The variable within a script has value only when the function is called for. That is, the variable defined within a script remains invisible until the function is called in the script. Remember, it is frowned upon to use many global variables in a script.

#Define a Variable that is visible throughout the script

#!/bin/bash

#Global Variable

COUNTRY="America"

#Defining the function called function_state

function_state()

{

STATE="ALASKA"

echo "The value of state is $STATE"

}

sleep 2

echo ""

echo "The value of two variables are "

echo "The value of country variable is $COUNTRY "

echo "The value of state variable is $STATE"

sleep 2

echo "Now, call the function"

#Calling the function, below

function_state

echo "See the difference."

sleep 3

echo "The value of country variable is $COUNTRY "

echo "AFTER THE FUNCTION called - The value of state variable is $STATE"

sleep 2

This script displays how variables are treated in the shell script. The variable that is defined first is called the "global variable" and the "variable inside the function" is called "local" variable and that gets a value only when its function is called.

You can also use functions to pass parameters from the command line. The parameters you pass to the function can, for instance, perform mathematical evaluations. If you are planning to learn Python, this section is useful for you.

Here is a currency calculator using functions and personalized for you. The personalization take splace, when you enter the parameter, in this case, YOURNAME, is the Global Variable. Next, you define a function, which calculates the rate from Japanese Yen to American Dollar.

```
$cat yen.sh
#/bin/bash

#Passing a parameter
YOURNAME=$1
#Define the function
function_yen()
{
echo "Hello, $YOURNAME, how're you today?"
echo "The current value of your Yen  is `expr $1 \* 111`"
echo ""
sleep 2
echo "Bye, have a nice day!"

}

#Interactive Read for input:
echo " Enter the US dollars you wish to convert:"
read USD
function_yen $USD
```

Expected output:

$ ./yen.sh Bobby

Enter the US dollars you wish to convert:

9999

Hello, Bobby, how're you today?

The current value of your Yen is 1109889

Bye, have a nice day!

You can infer several things from the previous script yen.sh.

The global variable is used in two ways. As a value captured from the command line as well as the first parameter for the function function_yen. However, there is a problem with the script as well, because invariably the value of Yen to Dollar is never an integer. At the time of the writing, it was 111.61 but **expr command** does not handle non-integers, and the script fails. You may investigate the **bc** command:

$bc <<< '9 * 11.9'

107.1

It is also the reason why Object Oriented programming languages like Python are gaining ground because they have simpler ways of handling floating numbers.

Interestingly, functions within a function can help you understand class and objects used in Python. It is a sort of a conceptual understanding which will be clear with the following example

```
$cat mendel.sh
#!/bin/bash
#This script is a take on Mendel's law

#Global Variable identifying the color of the pea plant

echo "What is the color of your pea Plant?:"
read COLOR

#Main Function

main_plant()
{
        FLOWER=1
        STEM=1

        funcRed()
        {
        ANTHERS=1
```

```bash
    echo " The Red Pea plant is male, it has $FLOWER flower
and $STEM stem with $ANTHERS Anthers."

    }



    funcWhite()
    {
     ANTHERS=0
    echo " The White Pea plant is female, it has $FLOWER
flower and $STEM stem with $ANTHERS Anthers."

    }

}

case $COLOR in
    "red" | "Red" | "RED")
    main_plant
    sleep 3
    echo ""
    echo "*******************************************************"
    funcRed
    echo "*******************************************************"
    ;;
    "white" | "White" | "WHITE")
    main_plant
    sleep 3
    echo""
```

```
        echo "***********************************************************"
        funcWhite
        echo "***********************************************************"
        ;;
        *)
        echo "Input either Red or White"
        ;;

esac
```

Explanation of the **mendel.sh** script:

This is the Global variable, COLOR, which is available throughout the script.

echo "What is the color of your pea Plant?:"
read COLOR

This is the Function that defines same characteristics of the plant.

main_plant()
{
      FLOWER=1
      STEM=1

This is the first nested function that defines specific character for the male pea plant.

      funcRed()
      {

```
ANTHERS=1

echo " The Red Pea plant is male, it has $FLOWER flower
and $STEM stem with $ANTHERS Anthers."

}
```

This is the second nested function for the female characteristic

funcWhite()

```
    {
     ANTHERS=0
     echo " The White Pea plant is female, it has $FLOWER
flower and $STEM stem with $ANTHERS Anthers."
    }
```

Note: The functions are defined first before the script. Why? Because functions do not do anything until they are called for!

This is the case statement that will read the value of the COLOR variable can take various variations of the phrase red

case $COLOR in

```
    "red" | "Red" | "RED")
```

Then the functions, **main_plant** and **funcRed** are called which get executed.

CHAPTER 15: AWK

Frankly, without knowing **awk,** it is difficult to survive in the Linux World. You need **awk** to make changes in the data and present it in a proper manner for mass consumption. The Sales guy is not going to churn numbers, all she/he needs is a presentation, graphs, bar charts and what not. You must dive deep into the world of data, create usable information that drives the business. Moreover, the fundamental tool to do it is awk.

Awk is used formatting text into useful information for a clear visual understanding, for printing specific columns, and it is excellent for searching and identifying data patterns. It also a full-fledged programming language with conditional statements. A good filter as well.

The primary syntax of awk is easy, it is mostly present in the **/usr/bin** directory, and this directory should be in your PATH name.

$which awk

/usr/bin/awk

The syntax is

$ awk '{ print <something> }'

For instance, imagine you are the IT personnel in a car dealership, and these are the sales figures for May for each Employee:

As you can see, it has three columns and eight rows, the headers are (Employee) no. , name (of the employees) and the number of cars they sold

$cat cars_sales_may.lst

No.	Name	Cars
201	John	10
202	Mary	11
203	Stephen	8
207	David	5
215	Ann	7
210	Peter	5

Identify, the first column by the following command:

$ awk '{print $1}' cars_sales_may.lst

No.

201

202

203

207

215

210

Note: Awk considers TABS as a natural separator.

The following example will show printing of the 2nd and the 3rd column:

```
$ awk '{print $2 $3}' cars_sales_may.lst
```

NameCars

John10

Mary11

Stephen8

David5

Ann7

Peter5

But the output looks bad, it has merged the fields. The reason is that you need a put an output format. You can try putting a comma and see if it helps:

```
$ awk '{print $2,$3}' cars_sales_may.lst
```

Name Cars

John 10

Mary 11

Stephen 8

David 5

Ann 7

Peter 5

Note: To dump the contents of the whole file use only $0 in awk

It does look better than the previous output, but still, you can do it better. You can to use double quotes and specify a space between the two columns, this is how you do it.

$ awk '{print $2 "   "$3}' cars_sales_may.lst

Name	Cars
John	10
Mary	11
Stephen	8
David	5
Ann	7
Peter	5

This is better than the previous output, but, still, you can do better. If you do not wish to see the headers in the first row. That is, we can eliminate the 1st row from the output using the NR variable. The NR is one of the most important variables in AWK. It stands for the number of Rows. So, as not to display the first row, the awk takes the following format of != or "not Equal to" used along with NR.

NR!=1

This is excluding the first row so that the command looks like:

$ awk NR!=1'{print $2 "   " $3}' cars_sales_may.lst

John   10

Mary   11

Stephen   8

David   5

Ann   7

Peter   5

Such is the power of NR which you can even specify the exact row you want by using == with NR.

$ awk NR==3'{print $2 "   " $3}' cars_sales_may.lst

Mary   11

Note: As with most Linux commands, you need to use the redirection symbol to save the formatted data into a new file.

$ awk NR==3'{print $2 "   " $3}' cars_sales_may.lst > new_-file.lst

But, what if you have a file that is not tab separated, for instance:

$cat systems.lst

server2:ubuntu:serverroom

server5:centos:serverroom

server8:suse:centralroom

This is just a file, with the names of the servers, the operating systems and their locations. Do you think, print $1, will display the first column? Let's try:

$ awk '{print $1}' systems.lst

server2:ubuntu:serverroom

server5:centos:serverroom

server8:suse:centralroom

The answer is NO. It, in fact, dumps the whole content like $0. The reason is that the awk considers only tab as the natural separator (or delimiter). And, for awk, the whole file seems to be a first column. Awk, has a provision for it, the option -F or field separator:

$ awk -F ":" '{print $1}' systems.lst

server2

server5

server8

Here, the field separator is : (colon), which is enclosed inside double quotes as shown in the example.

Now, using the same command structure, you can display multiple columns:

```
$ awk -F ":" '{print $1 "   " $3 }' systems.lst
server2   serverroom
server5   serverroom
server8   centralroom
```

Note: To introduce space and avoid merging of columns use "<space> <space> <space>" with the print statement.

Using the same systems.st file, you can filter data from the rows. Please be careful, while trying to learn these concepts, as they get confusing very quickly. Notice the placement of quotes, double quotes.

Awk takes the special conditions before {}, and the condition should be enclosed in single quotes.

In this, a file which separated by a colon, we want to display only the line -1nd row elements.

server2:ubuntu:serverroom

server5:centos:serverroom

server8:suse:centralroom

The awk command will be:

awk -F ":" '$1== "server2" {print $1 "   " $2}' systems.lst

$1 is the first column, by equating it to server2, we are displaying it the 1st row elements only. Since server2 is a string, enclose it within double quotes.

Make some changes in the original file, just adding the serial numbers:

1:server2:ubuntu:serverroom

2:server5:centos:serverroom

3:server8:suse:centralroom

awk -F ":" '$1==3{print $1 "   " $2}' systems2.lst

Here, notice that double quotes are not applied on 3.

There are other conditions that you can apply as well. For instance, looking at the car sales example:

$cat cars_sales_may.lst

No.	Name	Cars
201	John	10
202	Mary	11
203	Stephen	8
207	David	5
215	Ann	7
210	Peter	5

You want to know which employee as has sold more than 10 cars in May. Your awk syntax is.

Note: Note, we do not use FS here because it is a tab separated file

$ awk '$3>=10{print $2 "   " $3 }' cars_sales_may.lst

Name Cars

John 10

Mary 11

An even better result will be

$ awk '$3>=10{print $2 }' cars_sales_may.lst

Name

John

Mary

The condition applied to $3 or 3rd column is choosing values greater or equal to 10.

Awk can perform AND (&&) operations as well. Let's pull the May Car sales file again. You can two conditions, for instance, filter employee numbers greater or equal to 207 and those who have had sales of more than 6 cars.

No.	Name	Cars
201	John	10
202	Mary	11
203	Stephen	8
207	David	5
215	Ann	7
210	Peter	5

$ awk '$1>=207 && $3>6 {print $2}' cars_sales_may.lst
Name
Ann

Let's use this payroll file list now:

$cat payroll.lst

```
name:salary:supervisor:location:years
derek:40000:susan:usa:10
peter:60000:susan:australia:5
tony:45000:bobby:india:6
mizo:80000:park:japan:8
bobby:100000:susan:usa:20
kamlesh:1000000:Susan:20
susan:400000:walter:usa:25
```

It is obviously impossible to search for a pattern with either Row or Column numbers in a large file. Awk supports searching a pattern using the /<search_pattern/ methods before the print statement

$awk '/<search_pattern>/{print $0} <name_of_the_file>

$ awk -F ":" '/[sS]usan/{print $0}' payroll.lst

```
derek:40000:susan:usa:10
peter:60000:susan:australia:5
bobby:100000:susan:usa:20
kamlesh:1000000:Susan:20
susan:400000:walter:usa:25
```

Breakup explanation of the command:

awk -F ":" Defines the delimiter/separator Colon

/[sS]usan/ Looks for a search pattern that starts with either s or S and usan

print $0 applies for all records

payroll.lst name of the file

If you look at the file payroll again, you will see that Susan appears under name and supervisor. What if you are told to look at the record where Susan appears as an employee only, which is our first column

```
name:salary:supervisor:location:years
derek:40000:susan:usa:10
peter:60000:susan:australia:5
tony:45000:bobby:india:6
mizo:80000:park:japan:8
bobby:100000:susan:usa:20
kamlesh:1000000:Susan:20
susan:400000:walter:usa:25
```

You can specify only the first column in the following manner:

Take the previous example:

$ awk -F ":" '/[sS]usan/{print $0}' payroll.lst

And add the following option

$ awk -F ":" '$1~/[sS]usan/{print $0}' payroll.lst
susan:400000:walter:usa:25

You can use the ^ symbol to find records starting with a character, for instance if you wish to locate the pattern australia in the location column – which 4th column, you may try to use this command

```
$ awk -F ":" '$4~/a/{print $0}' payroll.lst
```
name:salary:supervisor:location:years
derek:40000:susan:usa:10
peter:60000:susan:australia:5
tony:45000:bobby:india:6
mizo:80000:park:japan:8
bobby:100000:susan:usa:20
susan:400000:walter:usa:25

The previous command searches for all instances of "a" in 4th column.

The correct command to use is as follows:

```
$ awk -F ":" '$4~/^a/{print $0}' payroll.lst
```
peter:60000:susan:australia:5

Let us to find pattern that occurs at the end of the line using $

```
$ awk -F ":" '$4~/a$/{print $0}' payroll.lst
```
derek:40000:susan:usa:10
peter:60000:susan:australia:5
tony:45000:bobby:india:6

bobby:100000:susan:usa:20

susan:400000:walter:usa:25

CHAPTER 16: SHELL COMMANDS THAT YOU MUST KNOW

The printf command

The printf command is used to display formatted text on the screen. If there is no preceding % before characters, they are printed as it is. Printf does not add a newline like **echo**, hence, use \n to add a new line. Any character which is preceded by a % is called a special character and the next argument is converted as per the specification. For instance, %d signifies integer. Hence, the next argument is treated as an integer.

$ printf "Hello"

The output will be without a new line, the $ at the end is the prompt.

$ printf "Hello"
Hello$

$print "hello\n"

Displays the output with the newline.

$printf "Hello, the next character will be an integer %d\n" 100

Hello, the next character will be an integer 100

The %d is replaced by 100

For instance, the special character specification %x is hexadecimal number. So, whatever number you enter after %x gets converted into its hexadecimal equivalent.

You can convert the %d which will be a followed by an integer into a hexadecimal number.

$ printf "Let convert %d to its hexadecimal equivalent is %x\n" 15 15
Let convert 15 to its hexadecimal equivalent is f

"f" is the hexadecimal value of decimal 15.

The alias command

This command is very popular among Linux users. It is like Windows shortcut. It is often put in the. .bashrc initialization file. In this example, the network is the shortcut for the common networking command ipconfig -a. Often, /sbin directory is not in the Path. Hence, you must put the full path of ifconfig, by using an alias now, you can type network to get the output.

$ alias network='/sbin/ifconfig -a'

$ network

enp0s3   Link encap:Ethernet HWaddr 08:00:27:fa:bf:86
        inet   addr:192.168.1.2   Bcast:192.168.1.255
Mask:255.255.255.0
        inet6 addr: fe80::1471:59ec:2c54:ccf6/64 Scope:Link
        UP BROADCAST RUNNING MULTICAST MTU:1500 Metric:1
        RX packets:510656 errors:0 dropped:0 overruns:0 frame:0
        TX packets:380241 errors:0 dropped:0 overruns:0 carrier:0
        collisions:0 txqueuelen:1000
        RX bytes:324920965 (324.9 MB) TX bytes:59476354 (59.4
MB)

lo   Link encap:Local Loopback
        inet addr:127.0.0.1 Mask:255.0.0.0
        inet6 addr: ::1/128 Scope:Host
        UP LOOPBACK RUNNING MTU:65536 Metric:1
        RX packets:1710 errors:0 dropped:0 overruns:0 frame:0
        TX packets:1710 errors:0 dropped:0 overruns:0 carrier:0
        collisions:0 txqueuelen:1
        RX bytes:152059 (152.0 KB) TX bytes:152059 (152.0 KB)

If you now enter the alias command, you can see that the last entry is the network alias. Some alias are created by default.

$ alias

alias alert='notify-send --urgency=low -i "$([$? = 0] && echo

terminal || echo error)" "$(history|tail -n1|sed -e '\"s/^\s*[0-9]\+
\s*//;s/[;&|]\s*alert$//'\")'"
alias egrep='egrep --color=auto'
alias fgrep='fgrep --color=auto'
alias grep='grep --color=auto'
alias l='ls -CF'
alias la='ls -A'
alias ll='ls -alF'
alias ls='ls --color=auto'
alias network='/sbin/ifconfig -a'

Note: You can open the .bashrc file to check the aliases you have by default.

The cut command

The cut command works best on data that are column formatted.

$uname -a

Linux linux1978 4.4.0-78-generic #99-Ubuntu SMP Thu Apr 27 15:29:09 UTC 2017 x86_64 x86_64 x86_64 GNU/Linux

If you want to pluck the 5th Character, which is the x of the word Linux, the cut command uses the option -c (for the character).

$ uname -a | cut -c5
x

To display a range of characters, use -c in the following manner:

$ uname -a | cut -c1-5
Linux

The grep command

The grep command searches for contents inside the files. It can search for a same pattern in one or more than one file at a time.

For example, you search "bash" in all the files in the current directory.

We use the wildcard expression * which stands for everything:

```
$ grep bash *
comp.sh:#!/bin/bash
country.sh:#!/bin/bash
for1.sh:#!/bin/bash
func1.sh:#!/bin/bash
func2.sh:#!/bin/bash
func3.sh:#!/bin/bash
getout.sh:#!/bin/bash
guess.sh:#!/bin/bash
```

The command output is in the following format
name_of_the_file:<what_you_serached_for>

By default, grep searches for case sensitive date, for example:

```
$ grep "susan" /etc/passwd
$
```

Fails to search for susan in the passwd file (This file stores user related information, in the real world, this file is no longer used)

But with -i option, grep can search for susan in /etc/passwd file.

```
$ grep -i "susan" /etc/passwd
Susan:x:1005:1005::/home/Susan:/bin/csh
```

To search for the exact word, use grep with -w option. Here is an example without -w example:

```
$ grep -w "bobby" /etc/passwd

Bobby:x:1001:1001::/home/bobby:/bin/csh
BobbyDeb:x:1002:1002::/home/bobby:/bin/csh
Bobbydeb:x:1006:1006::/home/bobby:/bin/csh
```

A helpful use of grep is when you can search for multiple options in one command line, this is possible by using -e option, look the following example:

$ grep -e "Bobby" -e "Susan" /etc/passwd

Bobby:x:1001:1001::/home/bobby:/bin/csh
BobbyDeb:x:1002:1002::/home/bobby:/bin/csh
BobbyDeb1:x:1003:1003::/home/bobbydeb:/bin/csh
Susan:x:1005:1005::/home/Susan:/bin/csh
Bobbydeb:x:1006:1006::/home/bobby:/bin/csh

The tar Command

They are various command available in Linux for archiving and compressions amongst which tar is the most popular. It is an easy command to use. The name tar is derived from the phrase "T"ape "Ar"chive. Tar is especially good in creating an archive consisting of multiple directories and files into a single file. It is commonly used to deliver software to costumers instead of shipping DVDs. Shipping DVDs may attract Taxes in some countries or US states. Such archives are commonly called tar-balls in the Industry. It is used with gzip command to compress the tarball. The gzip command is represented in tar with the -z option.

You can take the backup of your home using the tar command and its options -c (for CREATING) and it must be followed by -f , the next argument must be the tar ball you are creating and followed by *.* for all the files/directories your home, you can have a specific directory or a file as well.

$ tar -cf backup.tar /home/bobby

Note: To compress the data while creating an archive, put the -z option, for example

tar -czf backup.tar /home/bobby

You may get permission related errors, if some files are owned by the root.

Check if backup.tar is created

$ls -l backup.tar

To see the contents of the backup.tar without doing extracting it, use the -t option

$ tar -tf backup.tar

Note: The -f option has to followed by the tarball, otherwise you will get an error like

$ tar -ft backup.tar

tar: You must specify one of the '-Acdtrux', '--delete' or '--test-label' options

Try 'tar --help' or 'tar --usage' for more information.

To **extract** the contents, use the -x option. Please copy the backup.tar in some other directory and extract the contents in the following manner:

$ mkdir backup_tar

$ mv backup.tar backup_tar/

$ cd backup_tar

$ tar -xf backup.tar

Or better add -v for verbose

$tar -xvf backup.tar

If you don't have many files in the archive and wants to pick and choose which files you want to extract use the -w options with -x

Starts an interactive session like :

$ tar -xwvf backup.tar #Answer with either y or n

extract '1.sh'?y

1.sh

extract 'cars_sales_may.lst'?

extract 'comp.sh'?n

extract 'country.sh'?y

country.sh

extract 'error.log'?y

error.log

extract 'examples.desktop'?

CHAPTER 17: WHAT ARE REGULAR EXPRESSIONS?

It is an arduous journey. People may tell you that learning Shell Scripting is futile. That there is no future in it. This is a very superficial outlook. Do we stop learning mathematics which has theorems like Pythagoras written before Christ? How old is Shell Scripting? Surely, not old enough. The intention is to help you leap forward to learn the most popular programming/scripting language, and we sincerely believe that Shell Scripting is the way forward. Coming back to the topic, the Regular expression is the back bone of Shell Scripting, you must learn it. You cannot skip this topic, and it is really a tough nut to crack. Perseverance is the name of the game.

Regular expressions as you have seen in the chapters on sed and awk are used to search for patterns on a string. There are Four placeholders, two of which, we have already studied. To find the location of a pattern in a string at the beginning of the line, we use ^ (above 6 in the keyboard), to find the string at the end of the line, use $. The other two placeholders narrow it to words in a string, the beginning and end of the word anchors are /< and /> respectively.

Apart from the placeholders, you must know about character classes:

[xyz] matches either x OR y or z

[a-z] matches all characters from a to z but in small letters

[A-Z] matches all characters from A to Z in Capital letters

[^xy] does not match x and y

You may need to know how many users have bash or csh (C shell) as their default shell. You can find the information in the following manner:

First, put the value of the command

$cat /etc/passwd

Into a variable

$shells=$(cat /etc/passwd)

Check the value of shells variable

$echo $shells

Now, use the pattern match operator =~ to find the pattern csh in the string (which is nothing but the output of the cat /etc/passwd in the variable $shells)

On the prompt, type:

$[[$shells =~ csh$]] && echo "Yes, I found csh shells"

**$ [[$shells =~ csh$]] && echo "Yes, I found csh shells"
"Yes, I found csh shells"**

Now, try with a value of something you know doesn't exist in the /etc/ passwd file like ksh, the same command will not return anything.

Note: Now, please use the extended test [[ ]] .

www.ingramcontent.com/pod-product-compliance
Lightning Source LLC
LaVergne TN
LVHW051337050326
832903LV00031B/3594